CATHEDRAL MUSIC PRESS PRESENTS
WEDDING MUSIC FOR FLUTE & GUITAR

1 2 3 4 5 6 7 8 9 0

CATHEDRAL MUSIC PRESS IS A DIVISION OF MEL BAY PUBLICATIONS, INC.

Cathedral
MUSIC PRESS

Preface

Guitarists and flutists, like most musicians, often perform at weddings. Indoor, outdoor, formal, informal, sacred, secular, young people, old folks — the variety of celebrations is enormous. One common denominator, however, is that people care about the music played at this most important of events. It is my hope that this collection will provide flute and guitar duos with an effective and attractive repertoire for wedding ceremonies, and give prospective brides and grooms a happy musical alternative to the venerable church organ.

Wedding Music for Flute and Guitar is arranged in four sections — Prelude Music, Processionals, Meditations, and Recessionals. Some pieces may work well in several categories, and performers should select whatever they feel is appropriate for a given occasion. In general, the prelude pieces are longest, to accommodate tardy brides! The processionals have convenient stopping points so the music can end gracefully when the bride has reached the altar. Several of the meditations are religious in nature and several are not. The recessionals are long enough (some with repeats) to allow the bridal party to leave and people to mingle while still hearing music.

Many of the pieces in this volume are well-known works often associated with weddings; others, less familiar, were included for their musical content and mood. The transcriptions themselves are sometimes as literal as possible (as in the Bach pieces) and at other times quite free. While some of the works are presented in abbreviated form for optimum effect (Mendelssohn and Wagner), others have been kept intact in spite of the possibility of page-turning problems. The guitar parts are easy to intermediate level, with only occasional passages which may require some practice. While the guitar often provides accompaniment for the flute, I have tried, whenever musically possible, to give the guitarist some solo work or interesting figuration to play.

I would like to thank flutist Susan Thomas for her invaluable help in selecting the music, arranging the flute parts, and editing the manuscript, and for her encouragement throughout this project.

Mychal Gendron

Mychal Gendron

Mychal Gendron maintains an active schedule as a performer and teacher in the New England area. He has toured Brazil as a soloist under the aegis of Partners of the Americas, and has performed for ten years with flutist Susan Thomas as the Thomas-Gendron Duo. He has appeared as a solo recitalist, concertist, and chamber musician in all six New England states and at music festivals in Texas, North Carolina, and New Jersey.

A graduate of the North Carolina School of the Arts, Mr. Gendron studied with Jesus Silva, renowned guitar pedagogue and protégé of Andres Segovia. After studying in master classes with Alirio Diaz and Rey de la Torre he went on to earn a Master of Music degree in Performance from the New England Conservatory. He is now Chairman of the Guitar Program in the Rhode Island College Music Department.

Contents

Prelude Music

Processionals

Meditations

Recessionals

Prelude Music

Sleepers Awake
from Cantata 140

J. S. Bach
1685-1750

Allegro moderato ♩ = 72

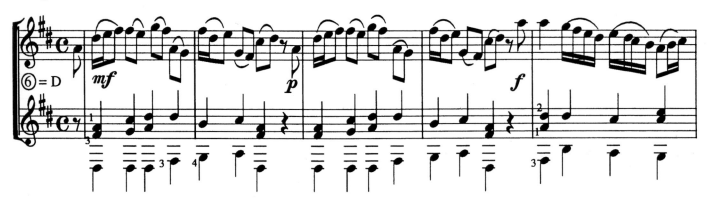

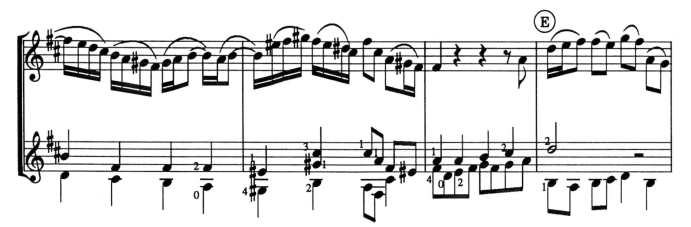

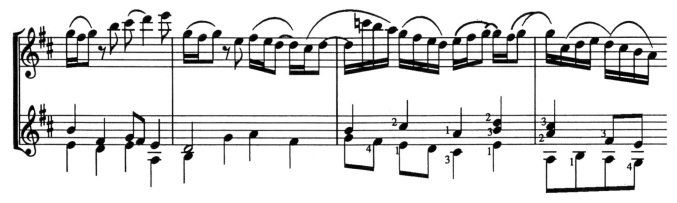

Sheep May Safely Graze
from Cantata 208

J. S. Bach
1685-1750

Andante pastorale ♩ = 56

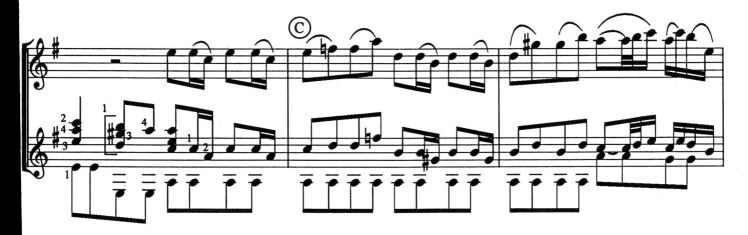

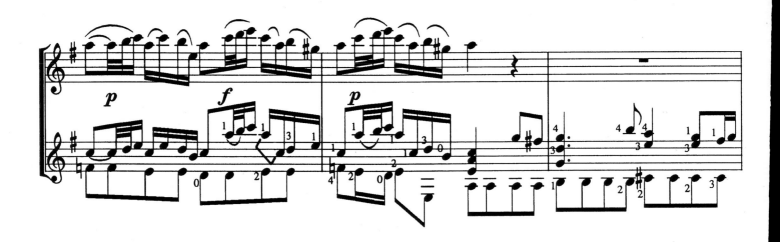

Meditation
from Thais

Andante religioso ♩ = 76

Jules Massenet
1842-1912

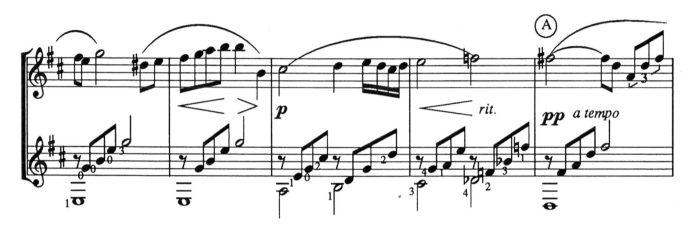

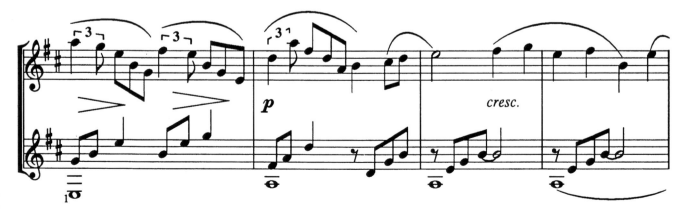

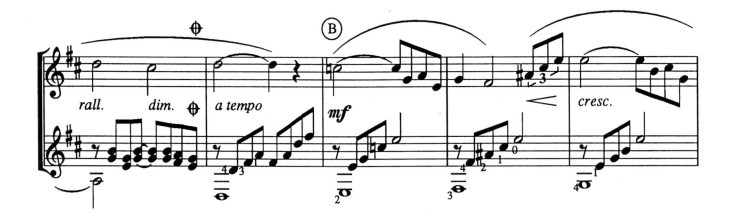

Poco piu appassionato

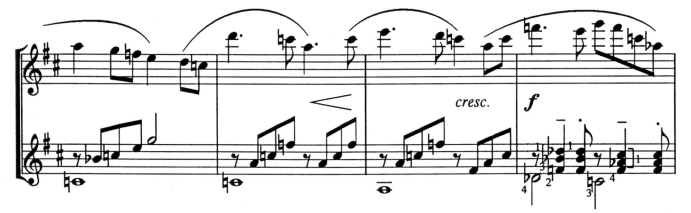

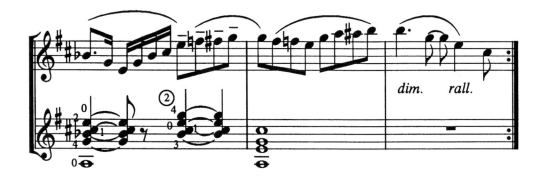

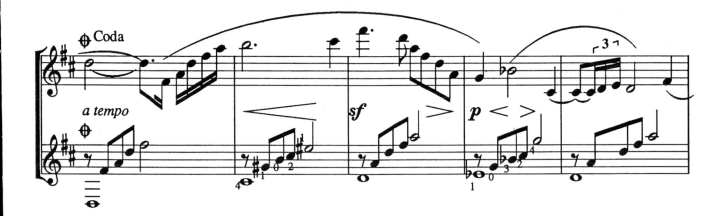

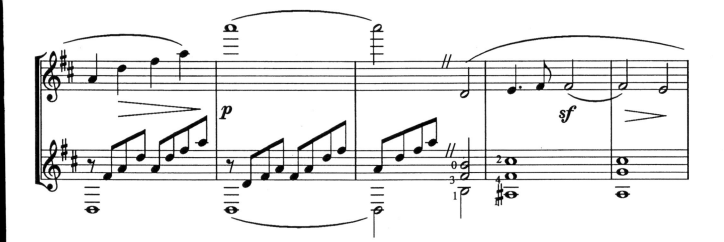

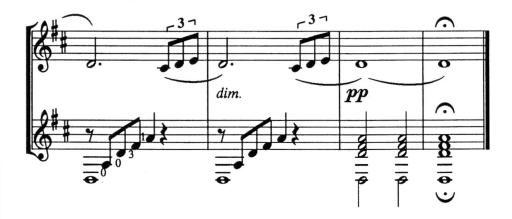

Ave Verum Corpus

W. A. Mozart
1756-1791

Adagio ♩ = 56

Processionals

Wedding March
from Midsummer Night's Dream

Felix Mendelssohn
1809-1847

Allegro ♩ = 63

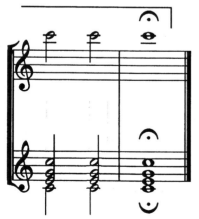

Rondeau
(Masterpiece Theatre Theme)

Jean Joseph Mouret
1682-1738

Moderato ♩ = 80

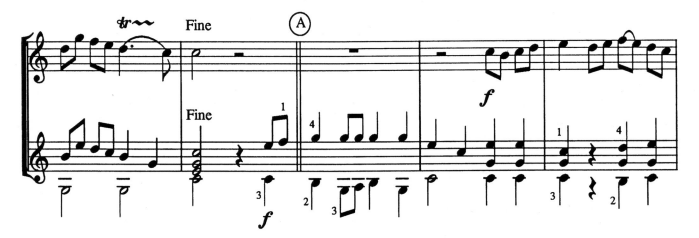

22

D.S. al Fine

24

Air

Andante ♩ = 88

John Dowland
1562-1616

Wedding March
from The Marriage of Figaro

W. A. Mozart
1756-1791

Andante ♩ = 100

Trumpet Voluntary
in D Major

Henry Purcell
1659-1695

Maestoso ♩ = 104

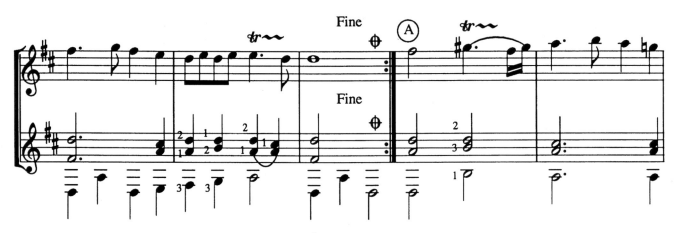

1. D.C.al ⊕ Coda

1. D.C.al ⊕ Coda

Ⓒ ⊕ Coda

Ⓓ

D.C. al Fine

Bridal Chorus
from Lohengrin

Richard Wagner
1813-1883

Maestoso ♩ = 69

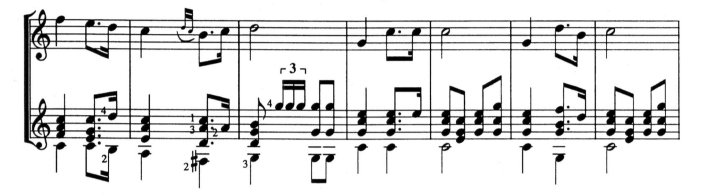

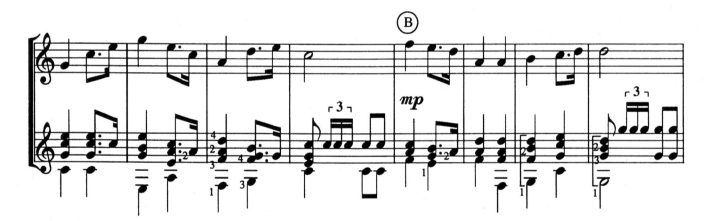

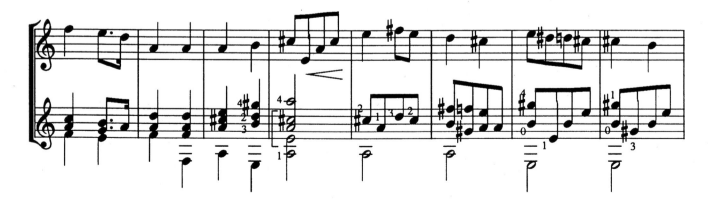

Meditations

Jesu, Joy of Man's Desiring

from Cantata 147

J. S. Bach
1685-1750

Moderato ♩ = 76

Ⓐ

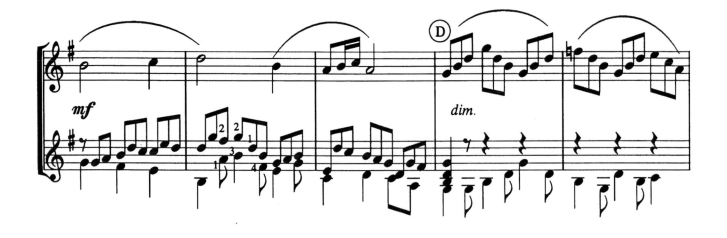

Ave Maria
on a prelude of J. S. Bach

Charles Gounod
1818-1893

Andante con moto ♩ = 72

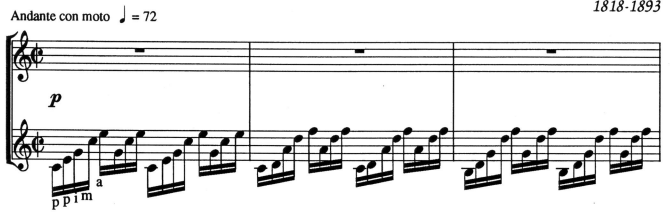

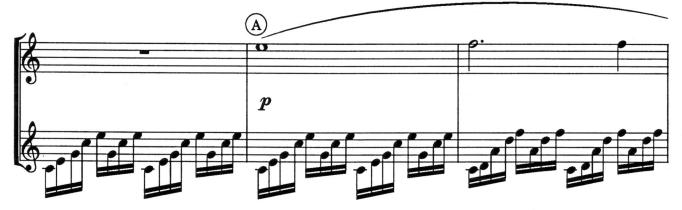

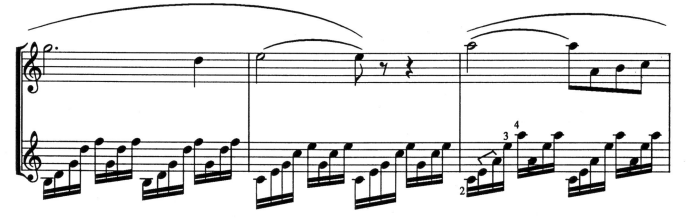

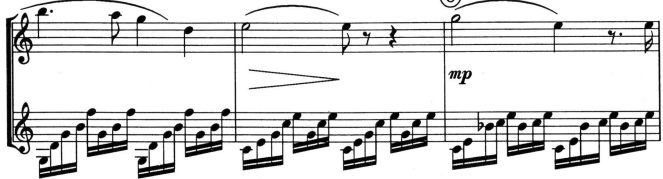

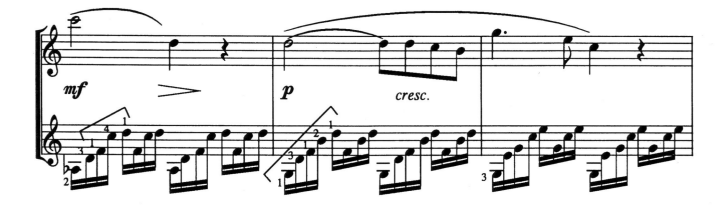

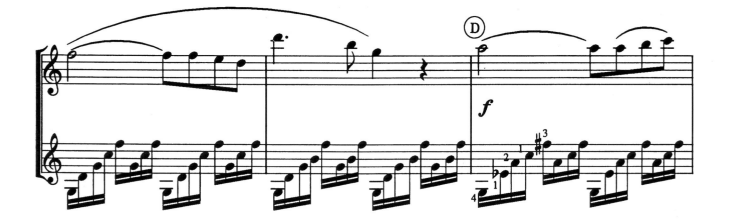

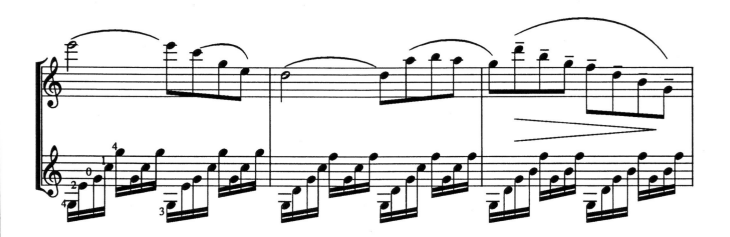

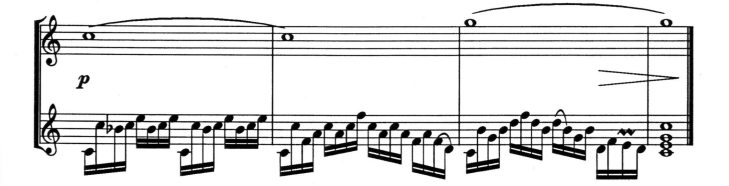

Evening Prayer
from Hansel and Gretel

Englebert Humperdinck
1854-1921

Andante ♩ = 52

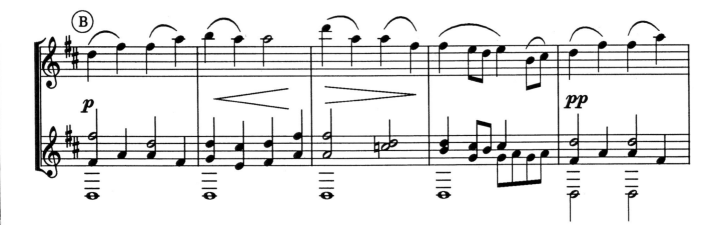

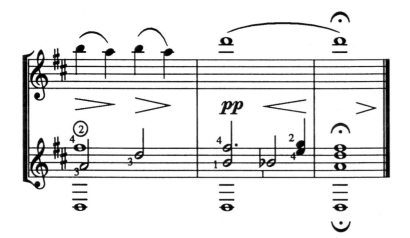

Ave Maria

Franz Schubert
1797-1828

Adagio ♪ = 56

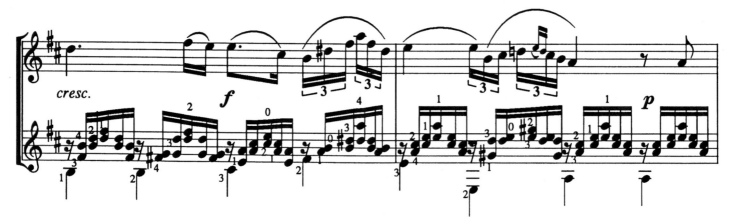

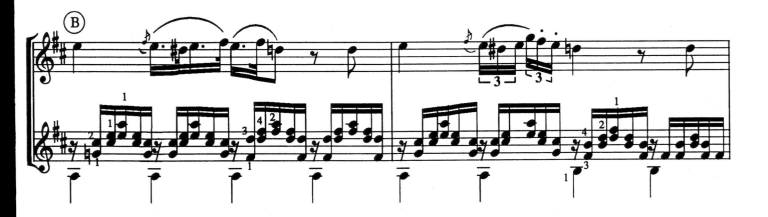

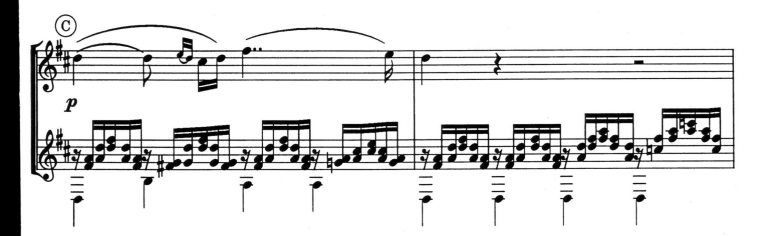

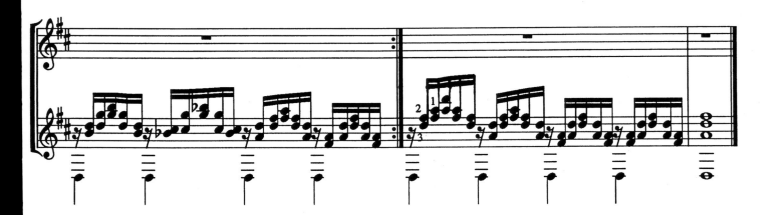

Traumerei

Robert Schumann
1810-1856

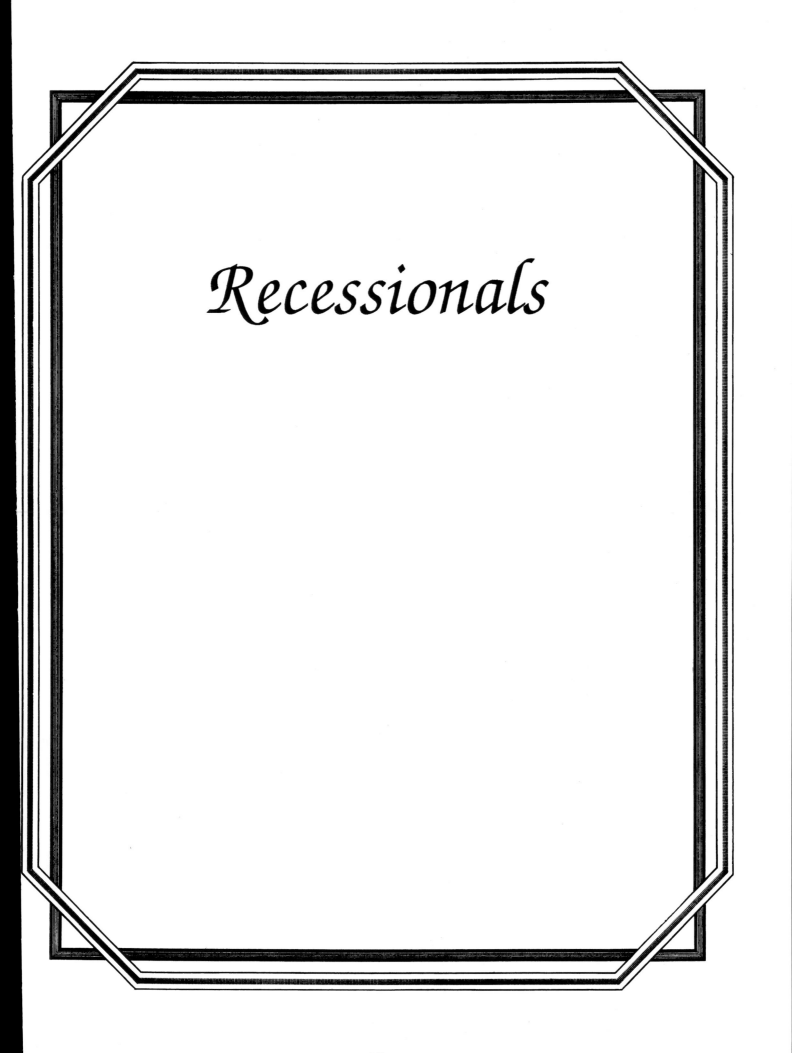

Recessionals

Air from Suite No. 5
The Harmonious Blacksmith

George Frideric Handel
1685-1759

Allegro ♩ = 63

Double I

Double II

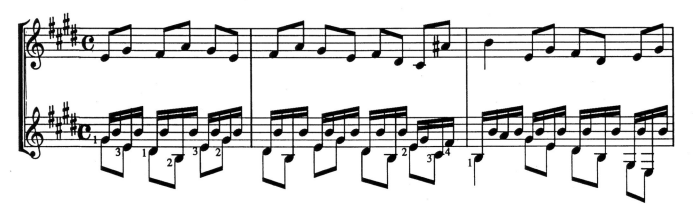

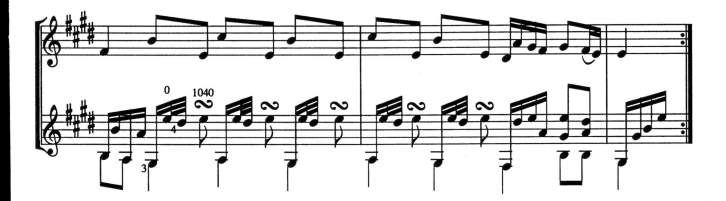

Double III

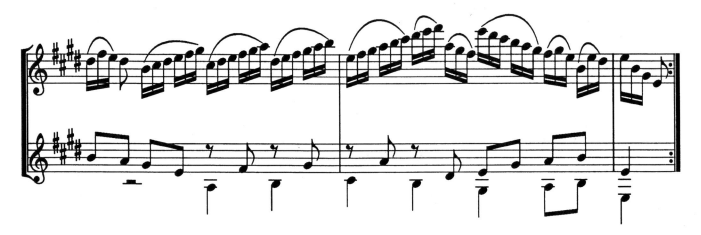

Double IV

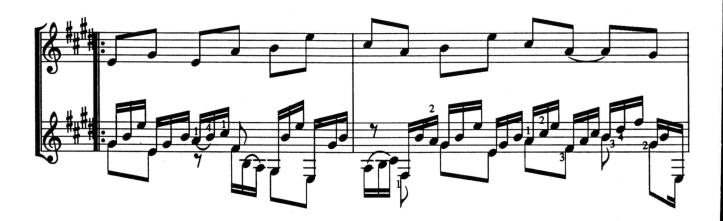

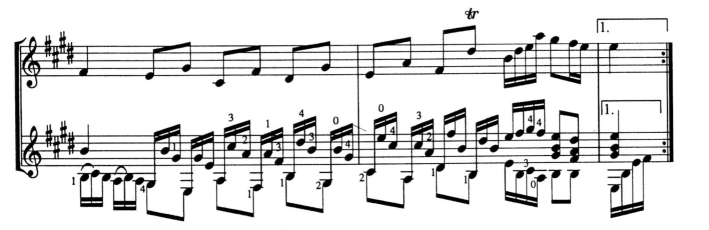

Alla Danza

from Water Music

George Frideric Handel
1685-1759

Allegro maestoso ♩ = 92

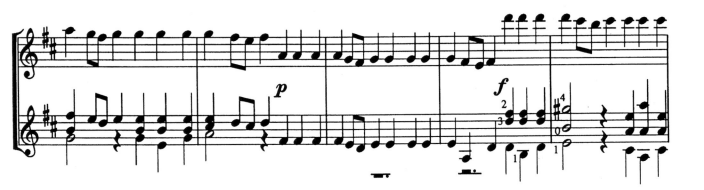

Fine

D. C. al Fine

Sinfonia
from Solomon

George Frideric Handel
1685-1759

Allegro ♩ = 92

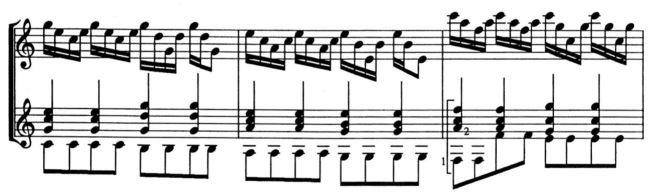

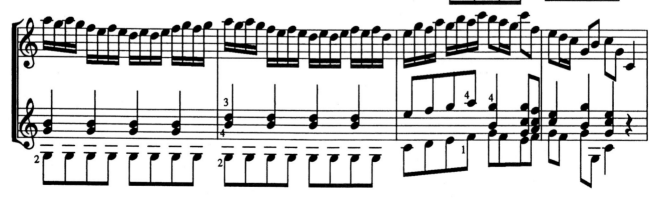

Bourrée

Michael Prætorious
1571-1621

Allegro ♩ = 88

Trumpet Tune

Henry Purcell
1659-1695